VOLUME ONE

INSPIRATION FOR CHRISTIAN LIVING

CHARACTER
COUNTS FOR
QUIET TIME
AND SMALL GROUPS

ROD HANDLEY

ELLIOT JOHNSON

GORDON THIESSEN

Character Counts for Quiet Time and Small Groups Volume 1

Rod Handley, Elliot Johnson, Gordon Thiessen

ISBN 1-929478-27-5

Cross Training Publishing
317 West Second Street
Grand Island, NE 68801
(308) 384-5762

This book is manufactured in the United States of America.

Library of Congress Cataloging in Publication Data in Progress.

The Fellowship of Christian Athletes logos, and "More Than Winning" gospel presentation used by permission.

Published by Cross Training Publishing,
317 West Second Street
Grand Island, NE 68801

CONTENTS

FOREWORD

BY DAL SHEALY

S everal years ago at a coaches forum, Bruce Bickel shared about 100 personality traits that coaches have and how a coach who understands these traits can better position his/her players and deal with their discipline, guidance, and motivation.

Following the coaches forum, Rod Handley and I began discussing a book based on these traits. The outgrowth of those conversations has now come to fruition with Rod, Elliott Johnson, and Gordon Thiessen uniting to write this book.

This book is an outstanding guide and tool for individual Bible study or small group study and discussion.

In this book you will find vignettes, questions, etc. all related to and supported with scripture. When we get honest with ourselves and with others, we can identify each of these character traits in our lives, and understand attitudes and personalities. As we do so, we acknowledge our assets and identify our liabilities so we can grow and become all God has created us to be.

Prayerfully, I hope and trust that this book will lead you to Jesus and enable you to grow and become all He has intended you to be as you walk the paths of life each day.

PREFACE

CHARACTER THAT COUNTS

We have a major problem in our society—a lack of character. Does character count? We say a resounding "Yes"—it does matter!! Over the past decade, we've attentively listened to people speak on the importance of character. By reading only public opinion polls, it's hard to determine if character truly matters anymore. We propose that character does count and that society is placing a higher premium on character. We see indicators of this as moral issues gain greater emphasis during political elections, in the media, from the pulpits, in the classrooms (public, private and home school education) and on the talk shows.

We're greatly concerned that character is lacking in society, especially when it involves people who claim to be Christians. There are numerous studies that indicate that Christians are as likely as non-Christians to falsify tax returns, to plagiarize, bribe, shift blame, ignore construction specifications, illegally copy software, steal from the workplace and selectively obey the laws of the land. Many believers have convinced themselves that their actions are justified, even though they are questionable and/or inappropriate.

Years ago, character development was learned early in life with a strong sense of right and wrong. People learned appropriate behaviors in the homes, schools and churches. Somewhere we lost it as we moved from developing internal character to focusing exclusively on external appearances, charisma and personality techniques. Success models were designed to help people achieve results without impacting the soul. In our nation we exchanged truth for a lie, and today we're reaping what we've sown with highest levels of immorality, drug/alcohol abuse, suicide, teenage pregnancy, abortion, murder, divorce and pornography.

We must be reminded that good character is simply based on Jesus Christ. A desire to emulate our lives after Him should be the goal of every Christian. When this happens genuine character takes root in our hearts and we become authentic. Unless true believers take this first step, we'll continue to see deterioration in our society because man-made character will crumble when faced with adversity and failure, while character developed and molded through Christ will stand.

The purpose of this book is to identify character qualities that will make a winning difference in your life. Make it your plan to examine at least one character quality each week. Read the short sports story, then do the **Pregame Talk, Warmup, Character Training, Go The Distance, The Finish Line and Character Quality**. The book is designed to interact with others in a small group setting. It can also be used as a family devotional. If you are leading a group, create an environment where you can freely exchange thoughts and ideas.

To get you started, here's a sample "Introduction" chapter. Enjoy the journey towards becoming a person of character.

PURPOSEFUL

A "PURPOSE DRIVEN" LIFE

Laura Wilkinson had real purpose when she competed in the ten-meter platform dive at the 2000 Olympics. After she won the gold medal, she was asked by NBC to put her emotions into words. "At first, I thought it was impossible," she said. "But I just wanted to go out there and dive for God and for everybody who ever dreamed."

Reggie White, one of the greatest football players of all time and a certain NFL Hall of Fame selection said, "I think that people who don't have a purpose end up dying twice. They don't know what they're going to do. I think that's why among ex-athletes, the divorce rate is so high because they left the game with no purpose. I have a purpose. Number one is my relationship with God and then family—my wife and kids. I want to spend more time with them. I want to go to their basketball games and band concerts." Reggie knows that people without Christ will perish.

How did being purposeful help Laura Wilkinson and Reggie White? How does having a purpose help you in life and in competition?

God inspired Solomon to write 3,000 proverbs and 1,005 songs (1 Kings 4:32). The book of Proverbs contains almost 1,000 of his sayings. The Proverbs are short sentences based upon his long experience. All are morally uplifting and easy to remember. All are scientifically accurate, for there are no fables found in God's Word. God had a number of purposes when He inspired Solomon to write the Proverbs. They include:

- To become wise
- To acquire understanding
- To receive instructions
- To become righteous
- To exhibit justice and equality
- To give prudence
- To gain knowledge and discretion
- To increase learning
- To listen to wise counsel

This book is written to help you become purposeful in your pursuit of character, gaining the wonderful benefits as noted in the Scriptures. The journey toward becoming a person of character is worthwhile. It has been said that ability may get you to the top, but character keeps you there. A person of character is marked by notable and conspicuous traits.

Character cannot be purchased. It's a quality of life lived. Horace Greeley said it this way, "Fame is a vapor. Popularity is an accident. Money takes wings. Those who cheer you today will curse you tomorrow. The only thing that endures is character."

God has a purpose for your life. Simply follow His leading and you can accomplish it. Big or small, if it is God's plan, it will be great. It's been said, "Expect great things from God. Attempt great things for God."

In the New Testament, Saul (the persecutor) became Paul (the bondservant) when his character was greatly transformed through an encounter with God on the road to Damascus (Acts 9:1-31). Later in his writings, we see in Philippians 3:10-11 that his sole purpose is to know Christ and to follow Him obediently.

The first step toward becoming a person of character is to get on the Lord's team. Turn to page 71-74 and make sure you're on the winning team before proceeding. As character takes root in your life, then you can confidently pursue God's purpose for your life. We'll be praying for you as you embark on this great journey.

1. What do you hope to gain as a result of going through this book?

2. Who do you know that has a definite purpose in life? Why did you select him/her?

3. How much of the Bible have you read and applied in the past? Is the Bible still appropriate today? Why do you feel this way?

CHARACTER TRAINING

Read the following Bible verses:

Job 42:2

"I know that you can do all things; no plan of yours can be thwarted."

Isaiah 46:10

"I make known the end from the beginning, from ancient times, what is still to come. I say: My purpose will stand, and I will do all that I please."

Micah 4:12

"But they do not know the thoughts of the LORD; they do not understand his plan, he who gathers them like sheaves to the threshing floor."

Luke 4:43

"But he said, 'I must preach the good news of the kingdom of God to the other towns also, because that is why I was sent.'"

1 Peter 2:21

"To this you were called, because Christ suffered for you, leaving you an example, that you should follow in his steps."

What do these verses tell us about the purposes of God? What does it mean to be "intent on one purpose"?

1. Is it possible to be a person of character without being a Christian? Why do you feel this way?

2. If you were given a nickname descriptive of your character, would you be proud of it? What character word best describes you?

3. Have you ever committed your life to Christ as defined on pages 71-74. If so, tell when and why you made this commitment? If not, would you like to do so now?

4. Would you describe yourself as a "purposeful" person? Why?

THE FINISH LINE

This week, write out and memorize Philippians 3:14:

CHARACTER QUALITY

The purpose of God's Word, including the Proverbs and Paul's writings, is that we might know Christ—the wisdom and power of God.

CHAPTER 1

CONFIDENCE

Sue Semrau, women's basketball coach at Florida State University, knows the importance of confidence. She says, "In athletics and in daily life, my players come up against many obstacles. I have tough conditioning requirements. We play in the ACC, and many of our opponents are ranked nationally." On February 8, 2001, FSU played the #4 ranked Duke Blue Devils on Duke's homecourt. During the game, Duke was ahead by 10 points during the second half, but Sue and her team rallied from behind to pull off a major upset. The key was not losing their confidence when they were down.

Sue tells her players often that confidence goes hand-in-hand with faith. If they have faith, they can remain confident. Faith is the foundation of self-confidence, on and off the court. Every day her players are bombarded with peer pressure and temptations. She tells them, "If you have faith in God, He will work through you and that will give you confidence, and confidence is richly rewarded."

Connie Mack was a great baseball manager, having led the Philadelphia Athletics from 1900-1950. Connie once made a great statement about confidence. He said, "I've seen boys on my baseball team go into a slump and never come out of it, and I've seen others snap right out and come back better than ever. I guess more players lick themselves than are ever licked by the opposing team!"

Describe a time when you exhibited great confidence. What was the final result? What words of wisdom can you gain from Sue's and Connie's perspective on confidence?

Elisha was a confident man who spoke the truth many times to God's enemies. An upset Syrian army was approaching with a plan to capture Elisha. Horses, chariots and a great army assembled by night around Dothan where he and his servant were located. Elisha's servant was petrified when he awoke and saw their opponents within easy striking distance. Certainly this would be the end. Yet when Elisha saw the enemy army, he remained confident. Why? Because he saw God's army assembled in greater numbers than the Syrians. Yes, God would prevail and He did.

Confidence in the Lord is crucial to our Christian walk. It is important that we remain unshaken, even when we go through trying times or when the obstacles appear overwhelming. Those moments when all seems hopeless are when we need to draw close to God and trust that He is able to accomplish His promises. Our confidence comes about because we realize that God is in charge of everything. Accept it or not, God's either in total control or He's off His throne. One of the indicators of spiritual maturity is a confidence that God is in control.

Too often we are dependent on the external things of life, which rise and fall like the stock market, to govern our relationship with God. That is not the way God designed it. As believers we have the unchanging, steady, indwelling presence of Jesus Christ. He can handle and solve anything. The internal control of Christ will lead you into a daily, deliberate walk with God. Whatever happens you turn over to Him, asking Him to sustain, strengthen and guide you. Such confidence and trust in Him stabilize your journey.

Good leaders ooze with confidence. Lord Montgomery wrote, "Leadership is the capacity and will to rally men and women to a common purpose, and the character which inspires confidence." Even if confidence isn't a part of your natural skill set, you can place confidence in God who is able to provide.

1. Who do you know that is full of confidence? What makes him/her a confident person?

2. What is something that you place confidence in? (For example, when you sit in a chair, you're confident it will hold you up or you may have confidence in certain people).

CHARACTER TRAINING

Read the following Bible verses:

Proverbs 3:5-6

"Trust in the LORD with all your heart and lean not on your own understanding; in all your ways acknowledge him, and he will make your paths straight."

Proverbs 3:25-26

"Have no fear of sudden disaster or of the ruin that overtakes the wicked, for the LORD will be your confidence and will keep your foot from being snared."

Psalm 71:5

"For you have been my hope, O Sovereign LORD, my confidence since my youth."

Micah 7:7

"But as for me, I watch in hope for the LORD, I wait for God my Savior; my God will hear me."

Hebrews 4:16

"Let us then approach the throne of grace with confidence, so that we may receive mercy and find grace to help us in our time of need."

What do these verses tell us about confidence? How do we obtain confidence? What happens to us as we become confident in God?

1. Describe an event or struggle during the past year when you decided to trust God. Are you glad you did? Why?

2. Are you a confident person? Why or why not? What is the basis of your confidence?

3. Ask God to reveal an area you are controlling that needs to be turned over to Him.

THE FINISH LINE

This week, write out and memorize Hebrews 10:23

CHARACTER QUALITY

We can live with great confidence because of who God is and because of what Jesus has done for us.

CHAPTER 2

DISCERNMENT

DISTINGUISHING GOOD VERSUS GREAT

Often, extreme sports such as skateboarding, surfing, biking stunt riders and rock climbing are viewed as being out of touch with their peers or, worse yet, they are painted as rebels or outcasts. In reality, many of these extreme sports bring out incredible athletic talents. Here are two examples.

Some people love tree-skiing...the art of skiing downhill weaving their way through a grove of standing aspen or spruce trees! But the sport requires much focus and discernment. Tim Etchells, a skier and writer, explains the technique. "Look at the spaces between the trees—the exits where you hope to be traveling," he says. Extreme-skiing world champion Kim Reichelm says matter-of-factly,

"Don't stare at what you don't want to hit."

Speed skydivers must also be very discerning. The sport requires a person to dive out of an airplane, stay streamlined like a bullet and pull the rip cords on the parachute within five seconds of splattering on the ground. Average terminal velocity for a free-falling human body is 110 mph, but speed divers can exceed 300 mph. As of November 1999, Mark Brooks, an expert speed skydiver, had made over 150 jumps and claimed the world record of 332 mph!

Do "extreme" sports appeal to you? Why or why not? Which ones have you participated in? What "extreme" sport would you never try? Why?

Prior to Jesus' public ministry, He was led into the wilderness to be tempted by Satan. After He had fasted and prayed for forty days, Satan approached Him three times with very enticing words and opportunities. Jesus responded with a scriptural answer to each of Satan's schemes. Notice that Satan even used scripture to try and trip up Jesus. Jesus was prepared to handle whatever was thrown at Him, no matter how appealing the temptation sounded.

Every Christian needs to have discernment to know what is true and what is false. We hear so many conflicting ideas today that we must discern what is from God and what comes from Satan. The Bible says we are to discern good from evil, right from wrong and the best from what is less than the best. How does this take place practically? Here are a few strategies I've tried to apply in discerning the proper response:

• Pray before reaching any judgment or decision. Ask God to reveal His truth to you.

• What does the Bible say about it? There are many areas where the Bible gives clear cut direction. Seek out a scriptural passage or biblical principle before applying man made answers. When the Bible is silent on the issue, then pursue the other items listed below.

• Seek out godly counsel. Trust me…you're not the first person who has encountered this situation. Consult with people you love and trust who can help you in your thought processes.

• Be a good listener as defined by James 1:19 "be quick to hear, slow to speak and slow to anger." Try to accumulate all the facts before you make a decision. Rushing into things without allowing your situations to work themselves out fully can create unnecessary disasters.

• Answer the following questions: What would Jesus do? Will this help me grow in my relationship with Christ? Will this bring greater glory to Christ? Will I be a better witness for Christ through this? Do I have peace about this?

1. Who is the most discerning person you know? How can you be more like him/her?

2. How discerning are you in distinguishing good from evil, right from wrong and the best from what is less than best?

CHARACTER TRAINING

Read the following Bible verses:

Proverbs 3:21-22
>   "My son, preserve sound judgment and discernment, do not let them out of your sight they will be life for you, an ornament to grace your neck. "

Proverbs 10:13
>   "Wisdom is found on the lips of the discerning, but a rod is for the back of him who lacks judgment."

Proverbs 14:6
>   "The mocker seeks wisdom and finds none, but knowledge comes easily to the discerning."

Proverbs 14:33
>   "Wisdom reposes in the heart of the discerning and even among fools she lets herself be known."

The verses above are just a few passages from Proverbs where discernment is addressed. Which of these verses help you understand the importance of discernment? What is the relationship between discernment, wisdom and knowledge in the verses above? How does correction affect the discerning person?

1. How can you be more discerning in situations at school? at home? in sports? on the job?

2. What are some of the strategies you should implement in becoming more discerning?

3. How do you currently handle the "gray" areas of life? What are the standards or guidelines you use to help you make correct decisions?

4. Ask God to help you be discerning in all of your decisions today to know what is the best.

THE FINISH LINE

This week, write out and memorize Proverbs 18:15

CHARACTER QUALITY

A discerning person thinks ahead about each decision and is sure to choose God's way, not his own.

CHAPTER 3

ENDURANCE

PERSEVERANCE—FINISHING THE RACE

Like a human torpedo shooting across the ice at 75 mph, luger Anne Abernathy has endured numerous broken bones, ruptured ligaments and torn tendons. She's endured nine knee surgeries and overcome years of lymphatic cancer treatment. She's also watched Caribbean hurricanes shred her home. Yet she still continues competing. While many lightheartedly call the oldest competing winter Olympian, "Grandma Luge," perhaps a better name is "Grandma Perseverance"—Anne will be 49 when she competes in the 2002 Olympics. Many of her competitors will be under 18. In spite of the obstacles of an aging body, this determined contender gives God the credit for her longevity in a winter sport where she often trains alone in her tropical homeland. "Clinging to God's Word has helped me get through. I look at perseverance as overcoming difficult times or overcoming hardship or resisting temptation," says Anne. "I wouldn't have perseverance if I weren't able to talk to God. I can't tell you how many times I'm on the treadmill or the bike just praying."

Describe a time in your life when you wanted to quit. What ultimately happened, and what did you learn from this experience?

Caleb and Joshua were the only two spies (of the twelve) who gave a positive report to Moses about the prospects of a successful invasion into the Promised Land. Forty years later because of their faith, Caleb and Joshua were the only ones allowed to enter the land. In Joshua 14, at 85 years old, Caleb still had a clear vision, an incredible passion and was ready to take action. He exclaimed, "I want this hill!" He is an example of a strong finisher—one who continued to trust and believe in God enduring to the end.

In 1968, the country of Tanzania selected John Stephen Akhwari to represent it in the Mexico City Olympics. Along the race course for the marathon, Akhwari stumbled and fell, severely injuring his knee and ankle. By 7:00 p.m., a runner from Ethiopia had won the race, and all other competitors had finished and been cared for. Just a few thousand spectators were left in the huge stadium when a police siren at the gate caught their attention. Limping through the gate came Akhwari, his leg wrapped in a bloody bandage. Those present began to cheer as the courageous man completed the final lap of the race. Later, a reporter asked Akhwari the question on everyone's mind: "Why did you continue the race after you were so badly injured?" He replied: "My country did not send me 7,000 miles to begin a race; they sent me to finish the race."

May that be our motto as believers in Christ. Not to just start the Christian race but to endure to the end. The Bible is littered with examples of men and women who didn't finish strong like Caleb. In fact, in a study done by Bobby Clinton from Fuller Seminary, he discovered that only 12 of the 49 most recognizable people in the Bible were strong finishers, maintaining a personal vibrant relationship with God right up to the end. May we be people of endurance, finishing strong right to the end of our lives.

1. Who is an example of endurance to you? Why did you select him/her?

2. Do you believe it is important to be a strong finisher? Why or why not? Would you describe yourself as a strong finisher?

CHARACTER TRAINING

Read the following Bible verses:

Psalm 100:5

"For the LORD is good and his love endures forever; his faithfulness continues through all generations."

2 Timothy 2:3

"Endure hardship with us like a good soldier of Christ Jesus."

2 Timothy 4:5

"But you, keep your head in all situations, endure hardship, do the work of an evangelist, discharge all the duties of your ministry."

2 Thessalonians 1:4

"Therefore, among God's churches we boast about your perseverance and faith in all the persecutions and trials you are enduring."

James 1:12

"Blessed is the man who perseveres under trial, because when he has stood the test, he will receive the crown of life that God has promised to those who love him."

Based on these scriptures, why is endurance an important character quality? Why are Christians urged to persevere through trials?

1. What do you believe are the keys to enduring?

2. If you died today, what would people say you contributed to society? What would you like carved on your tombstone?

3. What types of customs, traditions and attitudes do you want to pass on to your children and grandchildren?

4. Complete this sentence: In order to finish well, I need to

_____.

THE FINISH LINE

This week, write out and memorize Hebrews 12:7

CHARACTER QUALITY

The price of success is hard work, dedication to the job at hand, and determination that whether we win or lose, we have applied the best of ourselves to the task.

FRIENDSHIP

FRIENDS INFLUENCE AND IMPACT US

Charles Davis was 13 years old when Freddy, age 17, wanted him to break into a building and steal some typewriters. The older boy said he would be a lookout. Young Charles thought it over and told Freddy, "You go in. I'm going home." Six years later, Charles was a star basketball player for Vanderbilt University and he visited the state prison. There he saw Freddy for the first time since that night. He had been in prison since they had last met. "If I had gone in that building and got caught, who knows what would have happened to me, "says Charles, who played eight years in the NBA. Charles made a wise choice to get away from Freddy.

Tracey Hansen is a veteran player on the LPGA tour who recognizes the importance of choosing the right friends. She says, "I choose to spend the majority of my time with people who encourage me to stay true to my Christian beliefs, and I avoid close friendships with people who tempt me to do things I know are wrong. College friends and my friends on the tour have walked with me through the hard and fun times in life. But most importantly, they've helped me grow in my Christian faith. We meet weekly for Bible study, fellowship and prayer. I'm grateful for these relationships and for older mentors who show me how to stay strong in the Lord and how to experience His grace and comfort in good and difficult times."

What are some of the lessons that Charles and Tracey learned about choosing their friendships? Can you relate to their experiences? How?

David and Jonathan had one of the most remarkable friendships of all time. They met shortly after David killed the great giant Goliath. As the first born son of King Saul, Jonathan could've been easily threatened and jealous of David's popularity. Furthermore, David was destined to be the next king of Israel, not Jonathan. Yet Jonathan and David became tremendous friends, and the Bible describes the genuineness of their relationship as being "knit" together. Their commitment to one another was based upon mutual respect, compatibility and shared ideals. They wept together, accepted each other, encouraged and strengthened one another. An interesting sidelight to David's life is that the Bible doesn't have any record of David's sins until after Jonathan is killed on the battlefield. Subsequent to Jonathan's death is when David begins to get himself in trouble. Perhaps David could've spared himself much grief if he had found another friend to replace Jonathan.

Chuck Swindoll reminds us of four crucial truths pertaining to friendships:

• *Friends are essential, not optional.* There is no substitute for a friend—someone to care, to listen, to comfort, even to reprove.

• *Friends must be cultivated; they're not automatic.*

• *Friends impact our lives; they're not neutral.* Those we are close to rub off on us, change us. Their morals and philosophies, convictions and character eventually become our own.

• *Friends come in four classifications, not one.* They are: acquaintances, casual friends, close friends and intimate friends. Only with intimate friends do you have a deep commitment to mutual character development. You share the freedom to criticize and correct, encourage and embrace. They are your sheltering trees.

David and Jonathan were intimate friends who learned the power of a genuine friendship. Know a person's character before you make him a close friend. Your life is the stage on which his character—good or bad—will be played out.

1. What are your memories of your first best friend? What attracted you to him/her?

2. Who is your best friend currently? Why?

3. Would you describe your best friend as an intimate friend? Why or why not?

CHARACTER TRAINING

Read the following Bible verses:

Proverbs 12:26
    "A righteous man is cautious in friendship, but the way of the wicked leads them astray."

Proverbs 13:20
    "He who walks with the wise grows wise, but a companion of fools suffers harm."

Proverbs 24:1-2
    "Do not envy wicked men, do not desire their company; for their hearts plot violence, and their lips talk about making trouble."

Psalm 1:1
    "Blessed is the man who does not walk in the counsel of the wicked or stand in the way of sinners or sit in the seat of mockers."

1 Corinthians 15:33
    "Do not be misled: 'Bad company corrupts good character.' "

What do these verses tell us about friendships? What should be our attitude in seeking out friends? What are some of the dangers in having the wrong friends?

GO THE DISTANCE

1. Relationships have to be intentional...rarely do they happen without spending time together. Develop a creative list of ways by which you could initiate and improve friendships.

2. Who helps you to be a better friend? How does he or she do this?

3. John 15:12-13 reminds us to lay down our lives for our friends. Give examples of ways you have laid down your life for a friend, then give examples of ways friends have done the same for you.

THE FINISH LINE

This week, write out and memorize Proverbs 18:24

CHARACTER QUALITY

Your friends are like the buttons on an elevator. They will either take you up or take you down.

CHAPTER 5

GENEROSITY

GIVING IT ALL UP

Some people are kind and generous, while others are kind and GENEROUS! Linda Simmons, wife of former Oklahoma State head football coach Bob Simmons, is GENEROUS. In 1997, her husband faced near death because of kidney failure, but she graciously donated one of her own for a transplant. Three years later, Bob reflected saying, "God gives you miracles. He gives you certain people in your life to provide those miracles. To have a wife who showed unselfish love, what the marriage covenant meant, was nothing but a true lesson for me. We're closer because she's with me right now. I always carry her around with me. I think getting closer in my walk with Jesus Christ has really gotten me closer to my wife." Most of us won't have a chance to be generous the same way Linda Simmons did, but we can become generous in terms of our time, talents and treasures. Let's see specifically what God's Word has to say about money and possessions.

Discuss the generosity of Linda Simmons. Would you be willing to give a kidney if someone needed it? If so, would you do it for anyone?

The story of the rich young ruler and the woman who gave the Lord her last two pennies is an amazing contrast. The young man hoarded his possessions, while the woman gave all she had. The Lord was pleased with the woman's offering and had harsh words for the ruler.

The Bible has more to say about money than any other topic—over 2,000 verses worth. The way we handle money affects us spiritually, emotionally and physically. Contrary to popular belief, the Bible is relevant for today's economy and complex financial system. In His Word, God promises to provide all we need, and He does! The problems begin when we fail to manage the provision and resources carefully and we become lethargic to the principles God has designed for its use.

You can sum up God's principles into three truths: (1) *God Owns All You Have* - Psalm 24:1; Haggai 2:8; Deuteronomy 8:18. We are merely stewards. (2) *God Controls All You Have* - 1 Chronicles 29:11-12; Daniel 4:34-35. He is sovereign over all. (3) *God Provides All You Need* - Luke 12:30-31. He'll meet all your needs, not necessarily all your wants.

While many Christians think responsibility to God amounts to 10%, in reality all money belongs to God and we are simply caretakers of it. As stewards of these funds, we are responsible for properly managing it while we have it in our possession. God can decide to entrust us with as much or as little as He chooses. As stewards (not owners) of God's finances, it is our responsibility to be faithful managers. If we are faithful in our stewardship, God makes certain promises to us including peace, provision and prosperity. Freely give, and you will discover the joy of participating in God's grace.

One of the great joys in life comes from giving to those in need. And we always have something to give including our time, talents and treasures. Often the thing we take for granted may be a tremendous blessing to someone else.

1. Who comes to mind when you think of someone who is generous? Why did you think of him/her?

2. How would you define generosity in terms of giving of your time, talents and treasures? Which are the easiest and hardest for you to give?

CHARACTER TRAINING

Read the following Bible verses:

Proverbs 11:24

"One man gives freely, yet gains even more; another withholds unduly, but comes to poverty."

Proverbs 18:16

"A gift opens the way for the giver and ushers him into the presence of the great."

Proverbs 22:9

"A generous man will himself be blessed, for he shares his food with the poor."

Matthew 6:24

"No one can serve two masters. Either he will hate the one and love the other, or he will be devoted to the one and despise the other. You cannot serve both God and Money."

2 Corinthians 9:7

"Each man should give what he has decided in his heart to give, not reluctantly or under compulsion, for God loves a cheerful giver."

What does the Bible tell us about money in the verses above? Why do you believe God cares about money issues? What promises does God make to those who are generous and to those who are greedy? What results when generosity occurs?

1. How would you describe your philosophy on money: a spender, a saver, a tightwad, frugal, generous, "just charge it," coupons only or _____ (select one of your own)? When and how did you develop this philosophy?

2. How do you determine how much to give to your church, other ministries and those in need? How could you increase your giving?

3. If we are faithful in our stewardship, God makes certain promises to us including peace, provision and prosperity. Do you agree with this statement? Share a time when you were blessed because of your faithfulness.

4. What are your strong and weak habits or philosophies related to money?

THE FINISH LINE

This week, write out and memorize Proverbs 11:25

CHARACTER QUALITY

Jesus said it is better to give than to receive. We make a living by what we get—we make a life by what we give.

CHAPTER 6

GOAL-ORIENTED

TRUSTING GOD FOR BIG PLANS

Sports psychologist Thomas Tutko has helped many major league baseball hitters overcome the mental obstacles that rob them of confidence at the plate. Tutko stresses the importance of concentrating on the immediate task at hand. This way a player is not distracted, and his efforts are not divided. Rather than worrying about success and failure, the hitter must "calmly swing, relax, think about what he's trying to do, and thoughts of failure or success will be pushed out of his head by the business at hand." In other words, a single goal is needed.

Shelly Stokes was part of the U.S. Women's Softball team which captured the gold medal in the 1996 Olympic Games.

Stokes admits that John 3:30 is a verse that keeps her in check, "He must become greater; I must become less." "As a player on the U.S. team it can be real easy to lose my focus on why I'm here. There are many distractions and worldly things that get in the way. As athletes, we all go through difficult times when playing. Being able to know that God is greater than anything I can do helps make me relax and play for His glory. This verse helps me remember I need to keep God first in all I do."

How does having goals help you in sports? What are the consequences of not having a goal? What would you tell someone who has no goals identified?

Nehemiah was in grief for his exiled country and the destruction that had occurred in Jerusalem. He fasted and prayed, confessing Israel's sin to the Lord. God heard Nehemiah's prayer and appointed him to lead the efforts to rebuild the city walls. It was a daunting task, but Nehemiah had a plan. He and the people overcame numerous obstacles, and in fifty-two days they completed the walls. When the surrounding countries and enemies heard about the completion of the rebuilding effort, they were stunned. Certainly God had been in the midst of this lofty goal.

The most important thing about goals is having one. The purpose of goals is to focus our attention on them. Our minds will not reach toward achievement until clear objectives are identified. The magic begins when we set goals. It is then that the switch is turned on, the current begins to flow and the power to accomplish becomes a reality.

For many people, goals are established on January 1. Yet these new year's resolutions are often forgotten and obsolete by February 1. The best goals are those that are written down and reviewed regularly. Written goals confirm and formalize the process. By keeping them before you daily, you can stay current in evaluating your progress.

Allow God to be a part of your goal setting time. Trust Him for big things and the ability to stay focused. Commit yourself to establishing written goals and then believe God for the answers. When you seek God's plan first, all of your other plans will have a way of falling into place. Why not look to Him today for His answers—both for the innovative ideas you need and for the precise timing in which to implement them? Believe that God will either remove any obstacles in your path, guide you around it, or take you over it. Be assured that God will get you there—simply trust in Him.

1. How good are you at establishing goals? Do you put them in writing? How often do you compare your progress?

2. What goals have you set for yourself in school? in sports? on the job? with your family?

CHARACTER TRAINING

Read the following Bible verses:

Proverbs 15:22

"Plans fail for lack of counsel, but with many advisers they succeed."

Proverbs 16:9

"In his heart a man plans his course, but the LORD determines his steps."

Proverbs 19:21

"Many are the plans in a man's heart, but it is the LORD's purpose that prevails."

Proverbs 20:24

"A man's steps are directed by the LORD. How then can anyone understand his own way?"

James 4:15

"Instead, you ought to say, 'If it is the Lord's will, we will live and do this or that.' "

Based on these passages, why does God want to be involved in our goal setting? What happens when God is not a part of the process?

1. List the projects you would like to accomplish in the next month and year. What could you do to achieve them?

2. Respond to the following statements:
    * I would rather attempt to do something great and fail, than attempt to do nothing and succeed.
    * The only real limitations we encounter are those which we place on our minds!!
    * Set your goals high. If you aim for the gutter, that is where you will end up.
    * Desire alone is not enough. But to lack desire means to lack a key ingredient to success. Many a talented individual failed because he/she lacked desire. Many victories have been snatched by the underdog because he/she wanted it more. So if you desire—intensely—and you act upon it, then everything stands within your reach.
    * Take care of the possible and trust God with the impossible.

THE FINISH LINE

This week, write out and memorize Proverbs 16:3

CHARACTER QUALITY

Put your dreams into motion by setting God-sized goals and working toward them. Dreams coupled with hard work result in accomplishment.

CHAPTER 7

HUMILITY

KEEPING THINGS IN PERSPECTIVE

Darrell Green is one of the NFL's most outstanding cornerbacks and is still among the fastest even though he's in his forties. A seven-time Pro Bowler, he was named the NFL Man of the Year in 1996 and was awarded the Bart Starr and Ken Houston Humanitarian Awards. Green is the Redskins career interception leader with 44 career thefts.

When he entered the league in 1983, he was a young Christian, and he immediately surrounded himself with godly people. As a result, his faith and maturity in the Lord grew like a tree planted in fertile soil. His friends helped provide nourishment and the pruning he needed to help him continue to grow. He recently said, "I'm thankful for the maturing process that God continues to work in me as I grow in the fertile soil consisting of godly counsel, godly fellowship, time in Scripture and prayer. Of course, it's not always easy. I still fall short and people have to set me straight. There are many times I have to go back to a head coach, a position coach, a player, a friend, my wife or anyone else and humble myself and apologize for something I did." Darrell learned that humility before God and man allows character to be deepened.

What were some of the lessons in humility that Darrell Green learned? How have you learned to be humble?

If you've gained a favored position and find yourself relying on worldly accomplishments, remember who our example of humility is—Jesus Christ. Though He had equal status with God, He did not cling to His awesome perks. He set aside the privileges of deity and took on the role of a slave by becoming human. Then, just as amazing, he stayed human. It was an incredibly humbling process. He lived a selfless, obedient life, then died a selfless, obedient death. Because of His obedience, God honored Him far above anyone or anything else, so that all created beings in heaven and on earth—even those long ago dead and buried—will bow in worship before Jesus, calling out in praise that He is the Master of all, to the glorious honor of God the Father.

There are several principles that enable believers to honor God with a humble spirit:

• Listening allows us to hear what God, His Word, the Holy Spirit and others are trying to tell us.

• Self-examination allows us to prayerfully process decisions and events, helping us choose the right response.

• Confession allows us to cast off sin and guilt as we admit we're nothing without His strength, forgiveness, mercy and love.

Putting these three attitudes into practice as we follow Jesus Christ will definitely change the way we view success. It can be difficult to show humility when you're succeeding in life and living well. Maybe you're a stellar athlete, a computer genius or an outstanding artist. Maybe you're the one others always look up to. Considering yourself more important than others or bragging about your position in life sets you up for a fall. God wants you to be your best without being proud or arrogant. I love the old Native American saying, "When you were born, you cried and the world rejoiced. Live your life in such a manner that when you die, the world cries and you rejoice."

Genuine humility is what prompts us to give heartfelt thanks and to favor others more than ourselves. In summary, the two most important words: "Thank you." The most important word: "We." The least important word: "I."

1. Apart from Jesus Christ, who is the most humble person you
   know? Why did you select him/her?

2. Define humility. Is it possible to be humble in today's society? Why
   or why not?

CHARACTER TRAINING

Read the following Bible verses:

Proverbs 3:34
   "He mocks proud mockers but gives grace to the humble."

Proverbs 8:13
   "To fear the LORD is to hate evil; I hate pride and arrogance, evil
   behavior and perverse speech."

Proverbs 11:2
   "When pride comes, then comes disgrace, but with humility comes
   wisdom."

Proverbs 15:33
   "The fear of the LORD teaches a man wisdom, and humility comes
   before honor."

Proverbs 18:12
   "Before his downfall a man's heart is proud, but humility comes
   before honor."

   What do these verses tell us about humility? What does God give to
the humble? What does God promise to the proud? List some
characteristics of pride.

GO THE DISTANCE

1. Is it possible to balance confidence and humility? If so, how?

2. How can you live out "real" humility?

3. Try not to use the word "I" today. Every time it rolls off your lips, charge yourself a nickel. At the end of the day, give the money to a friend.

4. Would you be able to go an entire week without praising yourself? Try it out.

THE FINISH LINE

This week, write out and memorize James 4:10

CHARACTER QUALITY

Our role is to humble ourselves. God's role is to lift us up. If we do His job, He'll do ours.

CHAPTER 8

INTEGRITY

GOD IS INTO INTEGERS

The rules of golf are very precise and many good golfers are tempted to bend them. In 1987, Craig Stadler placed a towel on the ground before hitting a shot from beneath a tree. He said it was to keep his slacks clean, but he was declared in violation of Rule 13-2 which prohibits "building a stance." The penalty cost him $37,000. One golfer known for his impeccable integrity was Bobby Jones. Years ago, Bobby called a one-stroke penalty on himself, causing him to lose the U.S. Open by a single stroke! When praised for his honesty, he said, "There is only one way to play the game. You might as well praise a man for not robbing a bank."

Texas Tech women's basketball coach Marsha Sharp is known as a "lady of integrity." Her faith began as a child, was established in her teen years and continues to be nurtured as a adult. She said, "When you coach, your faith is helpful every day. There are a lot of challenges in how you choose to deal with people. Really, it's a mindset. One of the most important things to me is that I do not want to win if I can't win with integrity." The source of her integrity is her faith in Christ. Striving for integrity, Sharp desires to shape her players into more than winning athletes. She wants to develop them into champions for life. "At some point, they're going to have to quit playing, and they will have to decide what they're going to do with the rest of their lives."

Sports allow many opportunities to display integrity. When have you seen integrity demonstrated and when has it been lacking?

There are sixteen references in the Bible about integrity, and four of these occur in the book of Job describing his character. Job was a man who remained steadfast in his integrity in spite of the tests he faced.

Integrity comes from the Latin word *integritas*, which means wholeness, entireness or completeness. The root word "integer" is often used in math to represent a whole number, meaning untouched, intact and entire. Literally, integrity means you have a complete soul. It's not synonymous with ethical behavior, though ethics will often follow, but is more related to the whole concept of "being" rather than "doing." You don't attain true integrity through a series of behaviors (doing) but by being internally transformed through a personal relationship with Jesus.

God is into making integers; Satan is into fractions. God desires to bring people to wholeness, putting all the pieces together which will ultimately take place in heaven when we're united with Him. Satan, working through the vehicle of sin, tears things apart, dividing people, bringing confusion and conflict.

Remember, God's plan will ultimately succeed, and His universe will one day become one glorious integer (whole and complete). But until that happens, you and I must live in a fractional world and experience the problems that come from fragmentation.

Integrity must continually be built in our lives through the disciplines of our faith in Jesus Christ. We cannot place confidence in our own integrity and relax and become lazy, or we will soon regress into a pitiful state. Ted Engstrom said, "No matter how much we try to hide our actions, our integrity (or lack of it) always shows through." Integrity of character occurs when there is consistency between actions and inner convictions over time. Strong Christian character results from both human effort and divine intervention.

Become a person of integrity—one others will admire and emulate as you follow Christ's perfect example.

1. How would you define "integrity?" Do you think that "integrity" and "character" are the same?

2. Who is someone you respect because of his/her integrity? Why did you choose him/her?

CHARACTER TRAINING

Read the following Bible verses:

Psalm 7:8
   "Let the LORD judge the peoples. Judge me, O LORD, according to my righteousness, according to my integrity, O Most High."

Psalm 78:72
   "And David shepherded them with integrity of heart; with skillful hands he led them."

Proverbs 11:3
   "The integrity of the upright guides them, but the unfaithful are destroyed by their duplicity."

Proverbs 13:6
   "Righteousness guards the man of integrity, but wickedness overthrows the sinner."

Proverbs 29:10
   "Bloodthirsty men hate a man of integrity and seek to kill the upright."

   Which verse inspires you to pursue a life of integrity? Why? What are the benefits and blessings associated with a person who demonstrates integrity? How do you react towards those who live a life of integrity?

GO THE DISTANCE

1. Why is integrity important?

2. How is integrity demonstrated at school? at home? on the playing field?

3. What steps of integrity could you take to protect yourself from temptation?

4. How have you helped someone by demonstrating integrity? How have you honored God by demonstrating integrity? How have you blessed your family by demonstrating integrity?

5. How have you hurt someone by your lack of integrity? How have you hurt God by your lack of integrity? How have you hurt your family by your lack of integrity?

THE FINISH LINE

This week, write out and memorize Proverbs 10:9

CHARACTER QUALITY

Ability will enable a person to get to the top, but it takes character and integrity to keep him/her there.

CHAPTER 9

JOYFUL

Any athletic team has a great deal of happiness when it wins a championship—especially when it happens unexpectedly. The incredible elation of Bobby Thompson and the Giants following his home run to win the 1951 National League pennant is an example. So is Bill Mazeroski's seventh game, bottom of the ninth home run to give the Pirates victory in the 1960 World Series and Kirk Gibson's shot to win Game one of the 1988 Series. These heroics give "goosebumps" to all true baseball fans.

Happiness spills into other sports as well. When the United States beat the Europeans in the 1999 Ryder Cup, the golfers celebrated their comeback win by running onto the 17th green, much to the dismay of their opponents. When the Los Angeles Lakers won the 2000 NBA championship, their fans partied all night outside of the arena. Michelle Akers and her soccer teammates received world-wide acclaim when they won the 1998 World Cup. A tremendous jolt of excitement results when you win.

Notice in these stories that the emotions experienced could be described as joyful. But are joy and happiness the same? Read on.

Describe the most joyful celebration you've ever experienced. What made the moment so joyful?

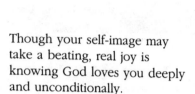

If anyone had reason not to be joyful, it was the Apostle Paul. In spite of numerous perils and persecutions, Paul remained upbeat and positive. His list of sufferings is identified in the passage above from 2 Corinthians and is more than most could bear. However, a Christian can experience genuine joy that isn't dependent upon outward circumstances. Those who are walking close to God can have joyful hearts no matter what happens to them. In contrast, what the world calls "joy" is better named "happiness." It comes and goes, depending upon external factors.

It has been said that happiness is when you are happy because of your circumstances while joy is when you are happy in spite of your circumstances. Joy can also be described as "feeling contentment and peace inside because God's in charge outside." Joy isn't based on emotional feelings or events. It is a deep, ongoing certainty and feeling of peace that no matter how rotten life is, God's still in control through every situation.

Though your self-image may take a beating, real joy is knowing God loves you deeply and unconditionally.

Paul Sailhammer says, "Joy is that deep settled confidence that God is in control of every area of my life." Tim Hansel believes, "Joy is not a feeling; it is a choice. It is not based upon circumstances; it is based upon attitude. It is free, but it is not cheap. It is the by-product of a growing relationship with Jesus Christ. It is a promise, not a deal. It is available to us when we make ourselves available to Him. It is something that we can receive by invitation and by choice. It requires commitment, courage and endurance." He also states, "Pain is inevitable, but misery is optional. We cannot avoid pain, but we can avoid joy. God has given us such immense freedom that He will allow us to be as miserable as we want to be."

There is no question that the day-to-day grind of life is difficult. In John 16:33 Jesus reminds us that in the world we will experience trouble. There will be tribulation, and we are not merely to endure it but to "be of good cheer" for He has overcome the world.

1. Identify several people whom you would describe as "joyful." What do you think causes them to be that way?

2. Discuss the differences between joy and happiness. Is it possible to have joy and not be happy?

3. What gives you the most joy?

CHARACTER TRAINING

Read the following Bible verses:

Proverbs 17:21-22
"To have a fool for a son brings grief; there is no joy for the father of a fool. A cheerful heart is good medicine, but a crushed spirit dries up the bones."

Psalm 16:11
"You have made known to me the path of life; you will fill me with joy in your presence, with eternal pleasures at your right hand."

Psalm 126:2
"Our mouths were filled with laughter, our tongues with songs of joy. Then it was said among the nations, 'The LORD has done great things for them.'"

Galatians 5:22-23
"But the fruit of the Spirit is love, joy, peace, patience, kindness, goodness, faithfulness, gentleness and self-control. Against such things there is no law."

What do these verses tell us about joy? Where does true joy come from? Do you believe that God is concerned about our joy? Why or why not?

1. What person in your family seems best able to cope with trouble and hardship? What is his/her secret?

2. Satan and the world will try to capitalize on every negative circumstance in your life to bring you down—to steal your joy. We must be forewarned and forearmed. What are some of the keys to keeping a positive attitude in the midst of difficult situations?

3. Living for Christ is the most dynamic, exciting and fulfilling journey you'll ever experience. How could you explain Christian joy to a non-believer?

THE FINISH LINE

This week, write out and memorize Nehemiah 8:10

CHARACTER QUALITY

JOY is spelled: JESUS OTHERS YOU in that order. When we put ourselves third, we have joy.

CHAPTER 10

KNOWLEDGE

LISTEN TO THE HEAD COACH

Tiger Woods totally dominated the 1997 Masters, virtually lapping the field as he won by a record 12 strokes. Yet when he reviewed the videotapes of his performance—blasting 300 yard drives, hitting crisp iron shots right at the pins and draining putts from everywhere, he wasn't satisfied. He confided in his friends that his swing was terrible.

Woods knew that he needed to overhaul his swing because if his timing was slightly off, he was susceptible to wild results. A new swing would allow him to hold his clubface square to the target for a longer period of time, decreasing the wild shots and increasing his accuracy.

With great determination, Tiger sought out his coach, Butch Harmon, to help him rebuild his swing. Harmon warned him that the results wouldn't come overnight—that Woods would have to pump more iron to get stronger, especially in his forearms. It would take months to groove the new swing. His tournament performance would get worse before it got better. It took a lot of courage for Tiger to seek out his knowledgeable coach.

In May 1999, something clicked on the practice range, and suddenly he realized that he had done exactly what he had been trying to accomplish. The victories followed. He won an extraordinary 10 of 14 events during the rest of 1999 and then followed up with another record setting season in 2000, amassing almost $10 million in winnings, including three major championships.

Who was/is your favorite coach? Why? What happened when you took his or her advice?

47

Throughout the entire book of Daniel, we see Daniel subjected to intense peer pressure and a value system which violated his views on God. Yet in the midst of it all, he remained pure and undefiled. He chose the right response to the situations he encountered. He exhibited great knowledge in all matters and God blessed him abundantly. What was the source of Daniel's knowledge? It was based on his intimate, loving relationship with God.

This is seen more fully in Daniel 6. The other leaders were jealous of Daniel, and they devised a trap to remove him from power. They put together a document which disallowed worship of anyone except their king. Was Daniel intimidated by their plans? Certainly not. He continued to kneel three times each day, praying and giving thanks to the one true God, just as he had previously done. He knew that when he knelt before God, he could stand before men. Daniel had grown in knowledge through his personal, private time before the Lord. In today's terms, Daniel had a consistent "quiet time."

What is a "quiet time?" I define it as time alone with God, allowing Him to speak to me through the Bible and communicating with Him through prayer. This intimate time with God is the key to deep Christian growth and maturity. Every committed Christian has this discipline as a core priority!!

The amount of time you spend is not the most important factor. Invest the first few minutes in preparing your heart in prayer. Then read your Bible. Pick a place to start (initially, I'd suggest the book of John), and then read consecutively—verse after verse, chapter after chapter. Don't race! Read for the pure joy of reading and allowing God to speak. You may want to also use a devotional book or a Bible study. The last few minutes should be set aside for prayer. Establish, renew or enliven your personal prayer time by giving God quality time each day. When you're actively reading and praying, knowledge will follow.

1. Who is the most knowledgeable person you know? How did he/she become so smart?

2. How can you gain more knowledge about how to live? about the world around you? about other people?

3. Who are some of your role models when it comes to a quiet time (parents, relatives, friends, teachers, roommates, etc)? What, if any, has been their impact on your life?

 CHARACTER TRAINING

Read the following Bible verses:

Proverbs 1:7
"The fear of the LORD is the beginning of knowledge, but fools despise wisdom and discipline."

Proverbs 3:19-20
"By wisdom the LORD laid the earth's foundations, by understanding he set the heavens in place; by his knowledge the deeps were divided, and the clouds let drop the dew."

Proverbs 10:14
"Wise men store up knowledge, but the mouth of a fool invites ruin."

Proverbs 11:9
"With his mouth the godless destroys his neighbor, but through knowledge the righteous escape."

Proverbs 17:27
"A man of knowledge uses words with restraint, and a man of understanding is even-tempered."

Which verse helps you best understand the value of knowledge? Why? Give examples when you've seen these verses lived out.

1. Who gave you your first Bible? How old were you when you received it? How did it influence your life?

2. Do you believe that the Bible is the source of all knowledge? Why or why not?

3. A quiet time can be defined as spending time alone with God and allowing Him to speak to you through His Word. Why is time alone with God a crucial foundation to character and personal spiritual growth?

4. Do you currently have a regular "quiet time"? If so, describe what you do. I urge you to strongly consider making this a daily discipline for the rest of your life.

THE FINISH LINE

This week, write out and memorize Proverbs 24:5

CHARACTER QUALITY

A wise person is always ready to listen and gain more knowledge.

CHAPTER 11

PATIENCE

SUCCESS COMES TO THOSE WHO WAIT

An old maxim says, "Success comes to those who wait." If we study the careers of famous athletes, we see that many have struggled through hard times before reaching great heights. For Babe Ruth, success was mixed with liberal doses of failure. In his career he belted 714 home runs but struck out 1330 times. Even the greatest NBA player of all-time, Michael Jordan, was cut from his high school basketball team. These men all had the patience to wait for success. They weren't afraid to fail along the way.

Mary Lee Tracy owns and coaches the Cincinnati Gymnastics Academy and has personally trained great champions such as Amanda Borden and Jaycie Phelps. Many years ago, Mary began working with a group of girls committed to winning the state meet, which they won within a few years. Then her goal was to instruct a national qualifier and to help someone earn a college scholarship; both of these occurred. Mary gradually climbed from a part-time coaching position to coaching the 1996 women's gymnastics gold medal Olympic team. She has learned many lessons along the way. She reflects, "I've learned that things happen in God's timing and you have to have patience. Sometimes His timing is fast, and sometimes we have to wait. During the slow periods there are more lessons I need to learn before God gives me the next step."

Do you an example of someone who exhibited extraordinary patience in their pursuit of success? When have you demonstrated great patience?

Hannah was a godly woman, but she had no children. She was greatly distressed by this situation, and she cried out to the Lord to provide a child. She vowed that if the Lord would provide, then she would give him to God and His service. Her patience resulted in God hearing Hannah's prayer; He granted her a son named Samuel. Samuel grew up to be a man devoted to the Lord and was instrumental in identifying Israel's first king and annointing a shepherd boy named David.

We live in an instant world—microwave ovens, the internet, cell phones and pagers—which has changed the way we view time. Standing in lines or being jammed in traffic send many people through the roof. A delayed airline flight can be aggravating. Overcrowded restaurants with two waitresses short gnaws on you. The ability to accept delays graciously, calmly and with a smile is tough. Speedy success is our expectation while learning to be patient is put on the back burner.

Does the fast paced world that we live in really bring meaning to our lives? What can we learn from having an attitude of patience?

Our lives need to be marked by patience. The Greek word translated "patience" literally means "long-tempered." There are three aspects to biblical patience: (1) Patience never gives in to negative circumstances, no matter how difficult. God told Abraham He would make him into a great nation and give Canaan to his descendants (Genesis 12:2, 7). When God made this promise, Abraham and Sarah had no children. They had to wait far past their childbearing years before God gave them a son. Abraham trusted God and patiently waited for Him to fulfill His promise. (2) Patience involves coping with difficult people. Paul tells us to "be patient with all men." (1 Thessalonians 5:14). This is a gentle spirit that refuses to retaliate. (3) Patience accepts God's plan for everything. It doesn't question God. A patient person says, "Lord, if this is what You have planned for me, that's all right."

1. Who is the most patient person you know? How do you see him/her demonstrating patience?

2. What are some of the lessons you can learn when you are patient?

CHARACTER TRAINING

Read the following Bible verses:

Psalm 37:7
"Be still before the LORD and wait patiently for him; do not fret when men succeed in their ways, when they carry out their wicked schemes."

Proverbs 14:29
"A patient man has great understanding, but a quick-tempered man displays folly."

Proverbs 15:18
"A hot-tempered man stirs up dissension, but a patient man calms a quarrel."

Proverbs 19:11
"A man's wisdom gives him patience; it is to his glory to overlook an offense."

1 Thessalonians 5:14
"And we urge you, brothers, warn those who are idle, encourage the timid, help the weak, be patient with everyone."

Why does scripture tell us the importance of being patient? Why are Christians urged to be patient with everybody?

1. In what circumstances do you need more patience?

2. Psalm 46:10 tells us to "be still and know that I am God."
   Chuck Swindoll says, "If we really want some things to count, if
   we genuinely desire some depth to emerge, some impact to be
   made, some profound and enduring investment to cast a
   comforting shadow across another's life (your child, a friend,
   whomever), it is essential that we slow down...at times, stop
   completely." What would happen if you followed this verse and
   Chuck's suggestion?

3. Don't rush through any task for the next 24 hours. Take your time.
   Later reflect on what you learned by not being in such a hurry.

THE FINISH LINE

This week, write out and memorize Proverbs 16:32

CHARACTER QUALITY

America's Prayer: Lord, give me patience...and I want it right now!!
God's Prayer: Wait on Me and I will deliver you.

CHAPTER 12

PRUDENCE

GRACIOUSLY HANDLING PRAISE

Going into the 1999 baseball season, Mike Sweeney was told by a coach of the Kansas City Royals that he had a zero percent chance of making the squad. Trade rumors were swirling throughout the off-season. During spring training Mike committed himself not to listen to the voices of other people but instead perform solely for the Lord. Much to the surprise of his coaches and teammates, Sweeney not only made the team, but he had a breakthrough year. He followed up the 1999 season by making the 2000 All-Star team and is now recognized as one the finest players in baseball. Mike has tremendous humility and great insight. He says, "I don't try to live up to anybody's expectations. You can't play that way. I've heard nice things about me before...all of us have to learn. Even when you're a success, everything is a learning process." Mike demonstrates a prudent attitude when receiving much praise.

Many people refer to Mike as the nicest guy in baseball. Royals President Dan Glass recently said, "Mike is simply the finest young man I have met or ever will meet in my lifetime. Such genuine character is hard to find with people in today's society. A world full of Mike Sweeneys is the closest to a perfect world it could get."

How do you handle criticism and/or praise? What does it mean to "perform solely for the Lord?"

Joseph had a roller coaster life. He was lavished, praised, exalted and honored at times. At other points in his career he experienced slavery, a prison sentence and loneliness. No matter what circumstances he experienced, he remained prudent ("sensible, sound judgment in practical matters"). After numerous ups and downs, he ultimately became the #2 man in all of Egypt where he had great influence and responsibility overseeing the food supply in preparation for seven years of famine. Because Joseph was prudent, Egypt was prepared for this potentially devastating situation.

Receiving praise and living up to the expectations of others can be a tremendous challenge. Former NFL quarterback Steve Pelluer had a great perspective when it came to reading the newspaper. He said, "I'm not nearly as good or bad as the press believes." Therefore he chose not to read the papers. He graciously handled praise, realizing he was only a few bad plays away from the "boo" birds. Steve knew first hand that he needed to play to an audience of One, not to the crowds or the media. God expects our best efforts in all of our activities. Whether on the job, in the classroom, on the athletic field, within our church or with our spouse, children and family, we are supposed to do our best for God's glory. God is our audience, not our employer, teacher, coach, pastor or spouse. When we remember that He is the one whom we serve, our performance can be centered solely on Him.

Before we become too impressed with our own accomplishments, we would be wise to remember that without God we can never achieve anything of lasting significance. Joseph and Mike Sweeney model this quality so well. No matter what's happening around them, they have their eyes focused on God. They know that being prudent has benefits both now and for all eternity.

1. Do you know somebody that you would describe as "prudent"?
   Why did you choose them?

2. How could being prudent help you?

CHARACTER TRAINING

Read the following Bible verses:

Proverbs 12:16
   "A fool shows his annoyance at once, but a prudent man overlooks an insult."

Proverbs 12:23
   "A prudent man keeps his knowledge to himself, but the heart of fools blurts out folly."

Proverbs 13:16
   "Every prudent man acts out of knowledge, but a fool exposes his folly."

Proverbs 15:5
   "A fool spurns his father's discipline, but whoever heeds correction shows prudence."

Proverbs 19:14
   "Houses and wealth are inherited from parents, but a prudent wife is from the LORD."

According to God's Word, what are some of the characteristics of a prudent person? How does a prudent person handle praise and/or criticism?

1. Talk about some of the ups and downs that you've experienced during your life. What did you learn from each?

2. What are keys to remaining focused on an audience of One?

3. What is one thing you could begin doing today in becoming a prudent person?

4. How can prudent behavior save you from much problems?

THE FINISH LINE

This week, write out and memorize Proverbs 22:3

CHARACTER QUALITY

Most of us would rather be ruined by praise than saved by constructive criticism. Prudent behavior will save you from much trouble.

CHAPTER 13

PURE SPEECH

CHOOSE YOUR WORDS CAREFULLY

The words we use to communicate have the power to build up or tear down. Steve Alford played under Bobby Knight at Indiana and then later spent a number of years in the NBA. Currently he is the head basketball coach at the University of Iowa. As a young Christian in college, Steve found it difficult to play for a coach who expressed himself inappropriately.

"The worst part of it, for me, was the profanity. I knew all the words—I hadn't led that sheltered of a life—but I had never heard them in such abundance and with so much fury behind them. To a young man of my background and religious beliefs, the vulgarity was like a punch in the stomach." Today, when Steve coaches, he is careful to choose his words—words that do not include profanity.

Steve is committed to helping student athletes understand that when you say and do things right, you can have a lot of fun.

Steve said, "Life is very exciting. You can live it in a very positive way and stay away from the negatives." When he first arrived at Iowa, he wrote all the state's high school basketball coaches urging them to challenge their players spiritually. Quoting from James and Ephesians, Alford talked about his own spiritual workout drills and his new chapel program for the Hawkeyes. He boldly told the coaches that winning is having a Christ-like spirit.

Have you ever played for coaches like the ones described above? How did you and your team perform under these differing styles?

James and Matthew both recognized the importance of our words and the need to control our tongues. Using the Lord's name in vain and profanity displeases the Lord as noted in the Ten Commandments (Exodus 20:7). Swearing is a lazy way of trying to be emphatic. Vulgar language is not appropriate in any situation. Expressing yourself in that matter proves absolutely nothing—except that you are a fool who has little grasp of the human language. Speaking inappropriately also involves half-truths (which are actually 100% lies), gossiping, bragging and talking without thinking first.

Speaking the truth "in love" can be challenging. You may have a tendency to hide your feelings, to pretend that nothing is wrong, while you silently brood over perceived or actual offenses. Then when you've hit the last straw, you explode like a grenade. The other extreme is to tell the truth but not do so in love. There may be nuggets of accuracy in the attacks you dish out, but if the truth is hurled like a weapon, it deeply wounds. Neither of these extremes breeds closeness.

If you tend to speak without love, to gossip, use profanity, exaggerate, to lie or to move your lips without first choosing your words carefully, consider the following suggestions:

• Think before you speak—just because you think of something, you don't have to say it! (Psalm 141:3; James 1:19, 26)

• Take wrong and inaccurate thoughts "captive" before God. Instead of blurting them out to others, confessing them to God helps get them out of your system and gives time to remind you of the truth. (Colossians 3:8-17; Proverbs 21:23)

• Replace these thoughts with new ones which more accurately represent the situation. (Proverbs 12:17-19; Philippians 4:8)

• Choose to speak edifying, pleasant words that are soaked in love. (Ephesians 4:29; Colossians 4:6)

The Bible tells us that even a fool may be thought of as wise when his mouth is kept shut (Proverbs 17:28). Silence can keep us from embarrassing ourselves. People may believe we are smarter than we really are!!

1. Who do you know that always chooses his words carefully and wisely? Why did you select him/her?

2. Which of the following areas do you have the most difficulty in controlling: profanity, gossip, half-truths, bragging or talking without thinking? Why did you select this one?

CHARACTER TRAINING

Read the following Bible verses:

Proverbs 11:12
   "A man who lacks judgment derides his neighbor, but a man of understanding holds his tongue."

Proverbs 13:3
   "He who guards his lips guards his life, but he who speaks rashly will come to ruin."

Proverbs 14:3
   "A fool's talk brings a rod to his back, but the lips of the wise protect them."

Proverbs 16:23
   "A wise man's heart guides his mouth, and his lips promote instruction."

Proverbs 21:23
   "He who guards his mouth and his tongue keeps himself from calamity."

Identify the truths noted in the verses above about the need for pure speech. Which ones really speak to you? How should we be using our mouths?

1. Have you ever been caught in a lie which spiraled out of control and eventually crashed? What ultimately occurred, and what did you learn from this incident?

2. What does it mean to speak the truth in love?

3. Complete the following sentence: In considering the biblical admonition concerning an "unbridled tongue" (James 1:26), I realize I need to . . .

THE FINISH LINE

This week, write out and memorize Proverbs 12:18

CHARACTER QUALITY

The best time to hold your tongue is when you feel you must say something or bust. People who guard their lips guard their life.

CHAPTER 14

SELF-CONTROL

REMAINING CALM AND COLLECTED

On August 28, 1956, Sammy White paid the price of a temper tantrum. The Red Sox catcher got so upset while arguing a play at home plate, he heaved the ball into center field—forgetting that it was still in play! Sammy was horrified to watch the Tigers' Red Wilson scamper from first base all the way around to score! Because of his frustration and his temper, Sammy White had cost his team a run that should not have scored.

LPGA Hall of Famer Betsy King has learned that one of the keys to being a successful golfer is to forget whatever happened on the last whole whether it's good or bad. Betsy describes one round where she was 7 under par after only 12 holes, and then lost the tournament by playing too conservatively. Another time, on one disastrous hole she twice hit the ball out of bounds, taking penalty strokes, and finished with a 10 on the hole and a 76 for the round. Her playing partner was amazed at her self-control. "But you have to put all that behind you," she suggests. "It's really hard, but you have to. And you can't compare yourself with others. That's where my faith in God helps me."

Describe a time in your life when you lost self-control. What resulted from your loss of control? Describe a time when you displayed tremendous self-control. What happened in this situation?

Moses was a man under control. Think about it...if you were Moses wouldn't you have given up on God's people over their continual whining, moaning and groaning? These people were so ungrateful, and they allowed themselves to get frustrated over all kinds of situations. They wanted out of Egypt yet when things got tough in the wilderness they wanted to return to slavery. They pleaded for food, but when God provided manna and quail—they didn't like it. They were skeptical that God would give them the Promised Land when the report of ten of the twelve spies came back negative. Moses somehow stayed above their cries and exhibited incredible self-control.

Remaining calm and collected in the midst of adversity, conflict, pain, disappointment and failure pleases God. Self-control is identified as one of the "fruits of the Spirit" (Galatians 5:22-23). One of my friends defined self-control as "love under control." Because of the love we have experienced first-hand from Jesus Christ, we can exhibit self-control rather than become angry or bitter. Therefore, the next time you find yourself in the midst of a difficult situation and you're about to explode, remember that self-control is the goal. In fact, Paul W. Powell reminds us, "God is more concerned about our character than our comfort. His goal is not to pamper us physically but to perfect us spiritually." Allow God the opportunity to mold and develop us; even when our comfort is at stake.

A great illustration of how irritation and pain can work to develop something beautiful is the oyster and its pearl. For an unknown reason, the shell of an oyster gets pierced and an alien substance—a grain of sand— slips inside. When it enters, all the resources within the sensitive oyster rush to the spot and begin releasing healing fluids which would otherwise remain dormant. As the irritant is covered, the would heals, developing a precious pearl. This jewel would have never developed without adversity.

1. Name a person who has great self-control. How does self-control help him/her?

2. What is an area relating to a person, place or thing that really frustrates you? How could exhibiting self-control make a positive difference in this area?

CHARACTER TRAINING

Read the following Bible verses:

Proverbs 19:2
   "It is not good to have zeal without knowledge, nor to be hasty and miss the way."

Proverbs 25:28
   "Like a city whose walls are broken down is a man who lacks self-control."

Proverbs 29:11
   "A fool gives full vent to his anger, but a wise man keeps himself under control."

2 Timothy 1:7
   "For God did not give us a spirit of timidity, but a spirit of power, of love and of self-discipline."

2 Peter 1:6
   "and to knowledge, self-control; and to self-control, perseverance; and to perseverance, godliness;"

From these verses, what difference does self-control make in a person's life? What traits emerge from a person who exhibits self-control?

1. Rather than complaining, try laughing when something goes wrong. What would happen if you adopted this attitude instead of becoming angry?

2. Our temper can get us into lots of hot water. Share a time when this happened in your life. What was the ultimate result of having a lack of self-control?

3. Do you become angry easily? What should you do when you become angry?

THE FINISH LINE

This week, write out and memorize Galatians 5:22-23

CHARACTER QUALITY

Self-control keeps us out of much trouble.

HAPTER 15

TEACHABILITY

KEEPING THE COBWEBS AWAY

Learning to be an outstanding athlete requires certain attributes as well as certain actions. First, a player must realize his/her current level of skill and identify where improvement is needed. This requires humility. Secondly, an athlete must be provided with good information from coaches who know the sport. Finally, the player must apply self-discipline and dedication to excel. This requires perseverance in practice. If a player refuses instruction, there is little hope for improvement. Most professional athletes will tell you that they achieved success in their sport because they were teachable, not because of their natural talents. They give credit to the coaches who helped equip them.

Lin Garrett noticed something special in an enthusiastic Cuban pitcher as he worked out for scouts a few years ago. Many scouts said he didn't throw hard enough, worried he couldn't get lefthanded hitters out and complained they didn't know his age. "But there was more to this guy," said Garrett. "He was taking ground balls at shortstop when a ball was hit foul into a parking lot; he sprinted after it and ran back with it. Who does that? No, this was a special type of person." This player was Orlando Hernandez, the Cuban "El Duque" who later became a major league star.

Who do you know who is teachable? Why did you select him or her? What character traits does a teachable person display?

Paul had a dramatic conversion to Christ on the road to Damascus, and his life was turned upside down. In the years that followed he gained great insights from the Lord. But Paul knew that he wouldn't live forever, so he urged believers to live out the truth of 2 Timothy 2:2, "And the things you have heard me say in the presence of many witnesses entrust to reliable men who will also be qualified to teach others." Paul poured his life into Timothy. Timothy was an eager, teachable student who not only studied under Paul, but who also accompanied him on his missionary journeys.

Chuck Swindoll tells us that our mind is a muscle. It needs to be stretched to stay sharp. He suggests three mental activities to keep the cobwebs away: (1) Read - Within the covers of a book are numerous ideas and insights waiting to be discovered. Read wisely, widely and slowly. Read history as well as current events...magazines and periodicals as well as classics and poetry...biographies and novels as well as the daily news and devotionals. (2) Talk - Conversation adds the oil needed to keep our mental machinery running smoothly. The give-and-take involved in discussion sessions, the question-answer dialogue connected to discussion provides the grinding wheel needed to keep us keen. Don't settle for surface talk. Dive into issues, ideas, controversial subjects, things that really matter. Ask and answer "why" and "how"...rather than "what" and "when." Socrates was considered wise—not because he knew all the answers, but because he knew how to ask the right questions. (3) Write - Start a journal. A journal isn't a diary; it's more. A journal doesn't record what you do—it records what you think. It spells out your ideas, your feelings, your struggles, your discoveries, your dreams. It helps you articulate who you are.

John Gardner once pointed out that by the time people are in their mid-thirties, most have stopped acquiring new skills and new attitudes. Make it a point to learn something new every day. Living and learning with a teachable spirit will add years and wisdom to our lives.

1. Who is the best teacher you've ever had? Why was he/she a good teacher?

2. Would you describe yourself as a teachable person? What is something you are currently learning?

3. Identify some of the books you have read in the last six months. What did you learn from them?

CHARACTER TRAINING

Read the following Bible verses:

Proverbs 4:1
"Listen, my sons, to a father's instruction; pay attention and gain understanding."

Proverbs 4:13
"Hold on to instruction, do not let it go; guard it well, for it is your life."

Proverbs 13:1
"A wise son heeds his father's instruction, but a mocker does not listen to rebuke."

Proverbs 16:20
"Whoever gives heed to instruction prospers, and blessed is he who trusts in the LORD."

Proverbs 19:16
"He who obeys instructions guards his life, but he who is contemptuous of his ways will die."

What do these verses tell us about the importance of remaining teachable? What should be our attitude toward wise instruction? How do you currently respond to instruction?

GO THE DISTANCE

1. How would you rate yourself pertaining to learning in the disciplines of reading, talking and writing? What could you do to improve in these areas?

2. Do something this week that you've never done before. What did you learn?

3. Are you a leader or a follower? If you're a leader, how could you improve in those skills? If you're a follower, are you following people who are godly examples?

THE FINISH LINE

This week, write out and memorize Proverbs 19:20

CHARACTER QUALITY

Because none of us knows everything about anything, we must remain teachable throughout life.

more than Winning
discovering GOD'S PLAN FOR YOUR LIFE

In most athletic contests, a coach prepares a game plan ahead of time. God designed a plan for our lives before the world began.

God is holy and perfect. He created us to love Him, glorify Him, and enjoy Him forever.

WHAT IS GOD'S STANDARD?

The Bible, God's playbook, says that the standard for being on His team is to:

Be holy.
"Be holy, because I am holy." - I Peter 1:16b

Be perfect.
"Be perfect, therefore, as your heavenly Father is perfect." - Matthew 5:48

WHAT IS GOD'S PLAN?

God created us to:

Love Him.
"Jesus replied: 'Love the Lord your God with all your heart and with all your soul and with all your mind.'" - Matthew 22:37

Glorify (honor) Him.
"You are worthy, our Lord and God, to receive glory and honor and power, for you created all things, and by your will they were created and have their being." - Revelation 4:11

Enjoy Him forever.
Jesus said, "...I have come that they may have life, and have it to the full." - John 10:10b

Why is it we cannot live up to God's standard of holiness and perfection? Because of...

Man's Problem

Man is sinful and separated from God.

WHAT IS SIN?

Sin means missing the mark, falling short of God's standard. It is not only doing wrong and failing to do what God wants (lying, gossip, losing our temper, lustful thoughts, etc.), it is also an attitude of ignoring or rejecting God, which is a result of our sinful nature.

"Surely I was sinful at birth, sinful from the time my mother conceived me." - Psalm 51:5

WHO HAS SINNED?

"For all have sinned and fall short of the glory of God." - Romans 3:23

WHAT ARE THE RESULTS OF SIN?

Separation from God.

"But your iniquities [sins] have separated you from your God..." - Isaiah 59:2a

Death.

"For the wages of sin is death..." - Romans 6:23

Judgment.

"Just as man is destined to die once, and after that to face judgment..." - Hebrews 9:27

This illustration shows that God is holy and we are sinful and separated from Him. Man continually tries to reach God through his own efforts (being good, religious activities, philosophy, etc.) but, while these can be good things, they all fall short of God's standard. "...all our righteous acts [good works] are like filthy rags." - Isaiah 64:6b

There is only one way to bridge this gap between God and man. We need...

God's Substitute

God provided the only way to be on His team by sending His Son, Jesus Christ, as the holy and perfect substitute to die in our place.

WHO IS JESUS CHRIST?

He is God.
Jesus said, "I and the Father are one." - John 10:30

He is Man.
"...the Word (Jesus) was God...The Word became flesh and made his dwelling among us." - John 1:1,14a

WHAT HAS JESUS DONE?

He died as our substitute.
"...God demonstrates his own love for us in this: While we were still sinners, Christ died for us." - Romans 5:8

He rose from the dead.
"...Christ died for our sins...he was buried...he was raised on the third day according to the Scriptures, and ...he appeared to Peter, and then to the Twelve. After that, he appeared to more than five hundred..." - 1 Corinthians 15:3-6

He is the only way to God.
"...I am the way and the truth and the life. No one comes to the Father except through me." - John 14:6

This illustration shows that God has bridged the gap between Himself and man by sending Jesus Christ to die in our place as our substitute. Jesus defeated sin and death and rose from the grave. Yet, it isn't enough just to know these facts. To become a part of God's team, there must be...

Replay of God's Plan

- ■ **REALIZE** God is holy and perfect; we are sinners and cannot save ourselves.
- ■ **RECOGNIZE** who Jesus is and what He's done as our substitute.
- ■ **REPENT** by turning to God from sin.
- ■ **RECEIVE** Jesus Christ by faith as Savior and Lord.
- ■ **RESPOND** to Jesus Christ in a life of obedience.

Jesus said, "...If anyone would come after me, he must deny himself and take up his cross daily and follow me." - Luke 9:23

Does God's plan make sense to you? Are you willing to repent and receive Jesus Christ? If so, express to God your need for Him. If you're not sure what to say, consider the "Suggested Prayer of Commitment" below. Remember that God is more concerned with your attitude than with the words you say.

SUGGESTED PRAYER OF COMMITMENT:

"Lord Jesus, I need you. I realize I'm a sinner, and I can't save myself. I need your mercy. I believe that you died on the cross for my sins and rose from the dead. I repent of my sins and put my faith in you as Savior and Lord. Take control of my life, and help me to follow you in obedience. In Jesus' name. Amen."

"...If you confess with your mouth, 'Jesus is Lord,' and believe in your heart that God raised him from the dead, you will be saved. ... for, 'Everyone who calls on the name of the Lord will be saved.'" - Romans 10:9,13

Once you have committed your life to Jesus Christ, it is important for you to...

Web sites with resources to help you grow in your faith:

www.fca.org
www.crosstrainingpublishing.com
www.characterthatcounts.org